Original Artwork Copyright © 1999 Ron D[...]
Text Copyright © 1999 The Brownlow Co[...]
6309 Airport Freeway ◆ Fort Worth, Tex[...]

All rights reserved. The use or reprinting of a[...]
this book without permission of the publisher is [...]

All scripture taken from the New International V[...]
and used by permission.

ISBN: 1-57051-400-3

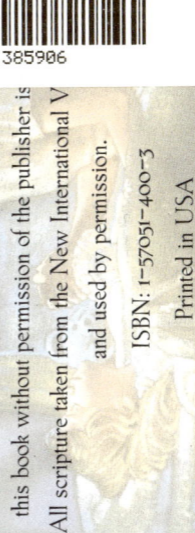

Printed in USA

A MOTHER PRAYS

101 Thoughts and Prayers

Compiled by
Caroline & Stephanie Brownlow

Brownlow

When the Fingerprints Are Gone

It will be gone before you know it. The fingerprints on the wall appear higher and higher. Then suddenly they disappear.

DOROTHY EVSLIN

★ A MOTHER PRAYS—101 ★

A prophet's tears, a mother's prayers, angels keeping watch... An artist whose heart is evident through the work of his hands, Ron DiCianni's paintings have been enormously successful in reaching and awakening the spirituality of thousands of art collectors worldwide.

A MOTHER PRAYS ✻ 100

Discovering an ability to love uncritically and totally has been exhilarating. It's the sort of love that calls upon my whole being, bringing all of my potential to life.

EASELETTES

A Blessing for Today ◆ Dear Daughter
Dear Teacher ◆ From the Heart of a Friend
Garden Gatherings ◆ Gardens of Love
Homespun Wisdom ◆ Reading the Greens
Song of the Thrush ◆ Thoughts for My Secret Pal
The Lord Is My Shepherd ◆ Words of Friendship

> *In motherhood, there's so much to learn, so much to give, and although the learning gets less with each succeeding child, the giving never does.*
>
> MARGUERITE KELLY AND ELIA PARSONS

A MOTHER PRAYS—99

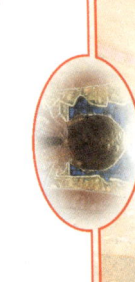

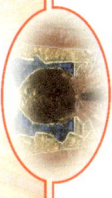

You, dear children, are from God.

I JOHN 4:4

My Loving Father, I can never thank You enough for the precious gift of my child...

✻ A MOTHER PRAYS—1 ✻

A MOTHER PRAYS

The pathway of life must be paved with praise. First to God and then to one another.

NANCY GORDON

Praise be to the Lord, for he showed his wonderful love to me.

PSALM 31:21

A MOTHER PRAYS * 2

It is in recognizing the actual presence of God that we find prayer no longer a chore, but a supreme delight.

GORDON LINDSAY

Dear God, too many times prayer has been a chore for me. Help me to see its joys and delights as we...

There are only two lasting bequests we can hope to give our children. One of these is roots; the other, wings.

HODDING CARTER, SR.

Dear God, I still need more roots and stronger wings, and I am supposed to give them to my child. Help me as I...

※ A MOTHER PRAYS—97 ※

Nowhere Else

How often we look upon God as our last and feeblest resource! We go to Him because we have nowhere else to go. And then we learn that the storms of life have driven us, not upon the rocks, but into the desired havens.

GEORGE MACDONALD

A MOTHER PRAYS—3

Before we can pray, "Thy kingdom come," we must be willing to pray, "My kingdom go."
ALAN REDPATH

God, I tried it "my way," and I am tired of it. Please take control of...

A MOTHER PRAYS — 4

A MOTHER PRAYS ✶ 96

*G*od pardons like a mother who kisses the offense into everlasting forgetfulness.

HENRY WARD BEECHER

*M*ay the Lord, who is good, pardon everyone who sets his heart on seeking God.

2 CHRONICLES 30:18, 19

A MOTHER PRAYS * 5

A Child Comes

A child enters your home and for the next twenty years makes so much noise you can hardly stand it. The child departs, leaving the house so silent you think you are going mad.

JOHN ANDRE HOLMES

The Importance of Today

Youth is the period of building up in habits and hopes and faiths. Not an hour but is trembling with destinies; not a moment, once passed, of which the appointed work can ever be done again, or the neglected blow struck on the cold iron.

JOHN RUSKIN

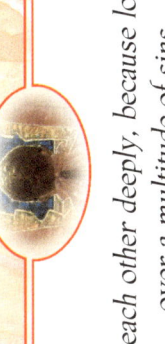

*L*ove each other deeply, because love covers over a multitude of sins.

I PETER 4:3

*T*here are only two things children will share willingly—communicable diseases and their mother's age.

✷ A MOTHER PRAYS—6 ✷

A MOTHER PRAYS • 94

I have lived to thank God that all of my prayers have not been answered.

JEAN INGELOW

Lord, I pray for Your will, not mine, to be done in…

A MOTHER PRAYS * 7

GOD, HELP US

O God, help us not to despise or oppose what we do not understand.

—WILLIAM PENN

HE HEARS OUR WHISPERS

*G*od puts His ear so closely down to your lips that He can hear your faintest whisper. It is not God away off up yonder; it is God away down here, close up—so close up that when you pray to Him, it is more a whisper than a kiss.

THOMAS DE WITT TALMAGE

A MOTHER PRAYS—93

God still speaks to those who take the time to listen.

Lord, I'm listening more now. Reveal Your will for our family in the area of...

★ A MOTHER PRAYS—92 ★

The Work of the Lord

Always give yourselves fully to the work of the Lord, because you know that your labor in the Lord is not in vain.

1 CORINTHIANS 15:58

★ A MOTHER PRAYS — 8 ★

A MOTHER PRAYS * 91

*W*e are apt to forget that children watch examples better than they listen to preaching.

ROY L. SMITH

*F*ollow my example as I follow the example of Christ.

1 CORINTHIANS 11:1

A MOTHER PRAYS • 9

Prayer must mean something to us if it is to mean anything to God.

ANONYMOUS

Dear Lord, these are not empty words, just going through the motions. Help me today to be a better mother in the area of...

Don't Run

Those who run from God in the morning will scarcely find Him the rest of the day.

JOHN BUNYAN

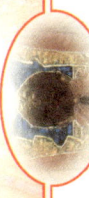

True Prayer

True prayers are like carrier pigeons: from heaven they came, they are only going home.

— Charles Haddon Spurgeon

A MOTHER PRAYS—10

A MOTHER PRAYS * 11

MOTHERING

Mothering should involve both taking care of someone who is dependent and at the same time supporting that person in his or her efforts to become independent.

SIGNE HAMMER

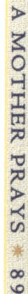

*L*evel with your child about being honest. Nobody spots a phony quicker than a child.

MARY MACCRACKEN

Father, please help me to be real and authentic with my child today, especially in the area of...

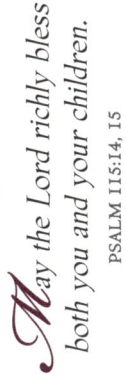

May the Lord richly bless both you and your children.
PSALM 115:14, 15

Lord, thank You for blessing us as a family. Please bless my child today in the area of...

A MOTHER PRAYS—12

A torn jacket is soon mended, but hard words bruise the heart of a child.

HENRY WADSWORTH LONGFELLOW

*D*o not let any unwholesome talk come out of your mouths, but only what is helpful for building others up according to their needs.

EPHESIANS 4:29

✺ A MOTHER PRAYS—88 ✺

I Never Knew

I never knew up to that time that God loved us so much. This heart of mine began to thaw out; I could not keep back the tears. I just drank it in... I tell you there is one thing that draws above everything else in the world and that is love.

—D. L. MOODY

Apart from God every activity is merely a passing whiff of insignificance.

ALFRED NORTH WHITEHEAD

Dear God, help me to talk to my child today about how much You mean to me, especially in...

A Prayer for Today

Here, Lord, is my life. I place it on the altar today. Use it as You will.

— ALBERT SCHWEITZER

A MOTHER PRAYS * 14

A MOTHER PRAYS ※ 86

No matter how old a mother is, she watches her middle-aged children for signs of improvement.

FLORIDA SCOTT-MAXWELL

May your mother be glad; may she who gave you birth rejoice.

PROVERBS 23:25

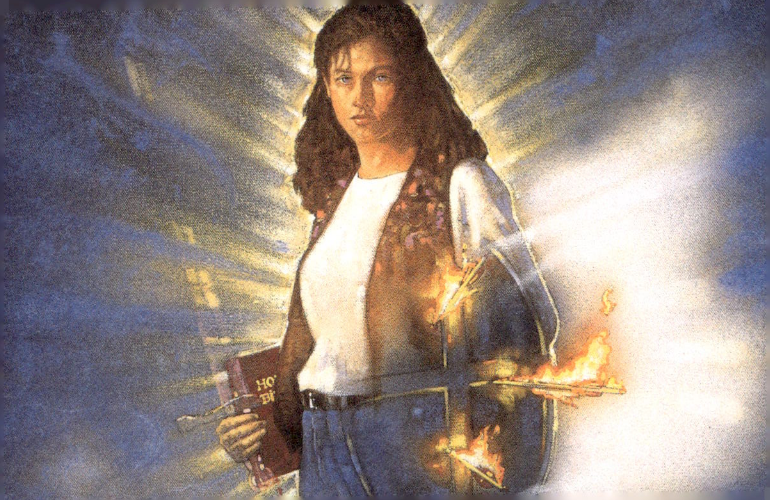

FOUR-LETTER WORDS

There's nothing wrong with using four-letter words in explaining the facts of life to children—words like love, kiss, help, care, give....

SAM LEVENSON

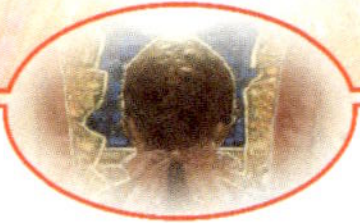

We're All Different

We are not hen's eggs, or bananas, or clothespins, to be counted off by the dozen. Down to the last detail we are all different. Everyone has his own fingerprints. Recognize and rejoice in that endless variety.

CHARLES R. BROWN

* A MOTHER PRAYS —15 *

A MOTHER PRAYS ✳ 84

*E*arth has no sorrow
that Heaven cannot heal.

THOMAS MORE

Father, You know our
family is struggling with....
Please help us to...

A MOTHER PRAYS * 16

I suppose there must be in every mother's life the inevitable moment when she has to take two small children shopping in one big store.

SHIRLEY JACKSON

*B*e joyful in hope, patient in affliction, faithful in prayer.

ROMANS 12:12

MOVING TOWARD GOD

Prayer is not an argument with God to persuade Him to move things our way, but an exercise by which we are enabled by His Spirit to move ourselves His way.

LEONARD RAVENHILL

A young child, ready for bed, interrupted a family gathering in the living room. "I'm going up to say my prayers now. Anybody want anything?"

ANONYMOUS

Lord, forgive me when I love Your gifts more than I love You…

A MOTHER PRAYS—17

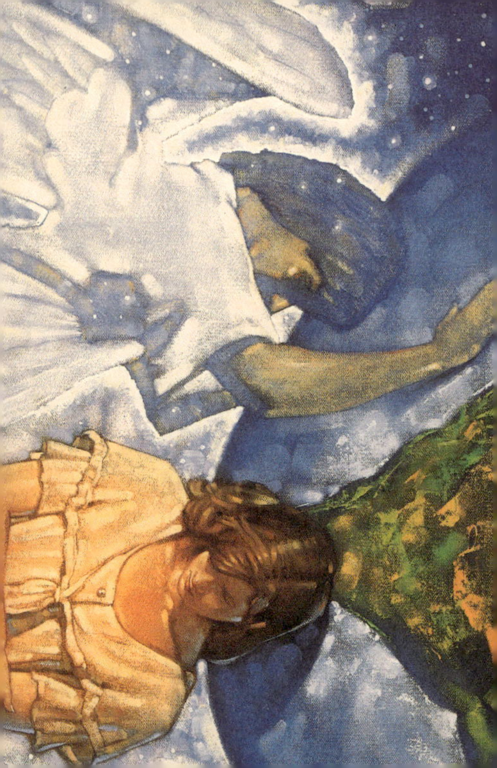

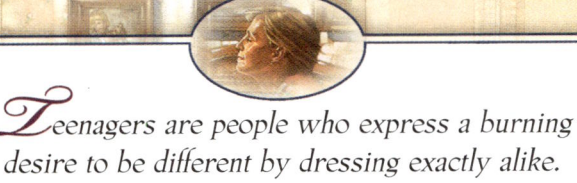

Teenagers are people who express a burning desire to be different by dressing exactly alike.

Do not conform any longer to the pattern of this world, but be transformed by the renewing of your mind.

ROMANS 12:2

★ A MOTHER PRAYS — 18 ★

A MOTHER PRAYS—82

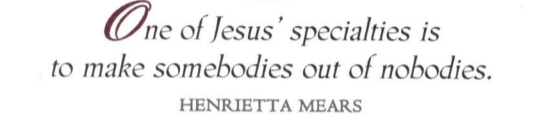

One of Jesus' specialties is to make somebodies out of nobodies.

HENRIETTA MEARS

Lord, I know my child is precious in Your sight and mine, but help me to show them their true worth comes from You, not their looks or clothes or IQ or...

A MOTHER PRAYS * 19

Nothing else will ever make you as happy or as sad, as proud or as tired, as motherhood.
—ELLA PARSONS

Dear Lord, You know how I feel today. I need Your strength to keep going as I face...

A MOTHER PRAYS ★ 81

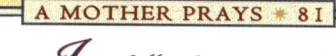

It is difficult to give children a sense of security unless you have it yourself. If you have it, they catch it from you.

WILLIAM D. MENNINGER

May those who love you be secure.

PSALM 122:7

Prayer and Trouble

*M*ost of us have much trouble praying when we are in little trouble, but we have little trouble praying when we are in much trouble.

RICHARD P. COOK

A MOTHER PRAYS—20

God Is Awake

Have courage for the great sorrows of life and patience for the small ones; and when you have laboriously accomplished your daily task, go to sleep in peace. God is awake.

VICTOR HUGO

A MOTHER PRAYS ★ 21

BEING A MOM

Being a mother, as far as I can tell, is a constantly evolving process of adapting to the needs of your child while also changing and growing as a person in your own right.

DEBORAH INSEL

A MOTHER PRAYS ★ 79

A MOTHER IS GOD'S LOVE IN ACTION.

Lord, You've placed an extremely high expectation on mothers. Help me to convey Your love today as we...

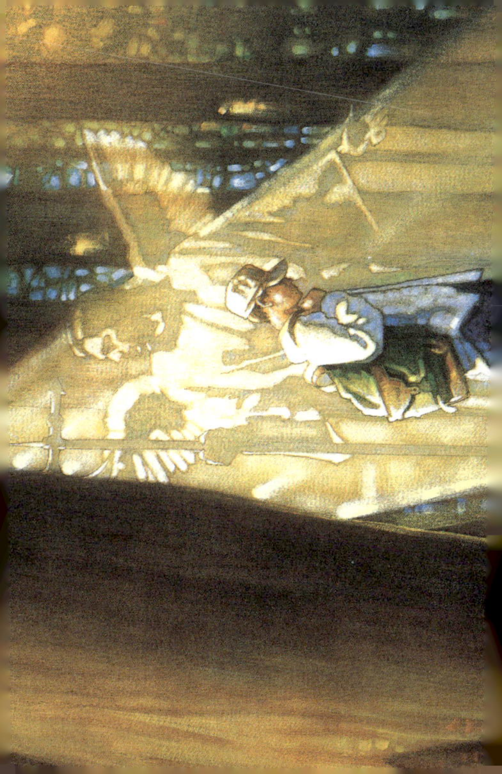

We parents can often do more for our children by correcting our own faults than by trying to correct theirs.

Blessed is the man whom God corrects.

JOB 5:17

A MOTHER PRAYS—78

Good Morning, Lord

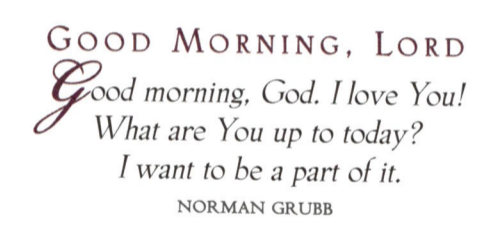

Good morning, God. I love You! What are You up to today? I want to be a part of it.

NORMAN GRUBB

A MOTHER PRAYS—22

The Lord gives His blessing when He finds the vessel empty.

THOMAS À KEMPIS

Lord, I confess my emptiness. I need Your power today in dealing with my child's....

A MOTHER PRAYS—77

Blessed Are They

Blessed are those who see the hand of God in the haphazard, inexplicable, and seemingly senseless circumstances of life.

ERWIN W. LUTZER

★ A MOTHER PRAYS — 23 ★

MIRACULOUS LOVE

Maternal love: a miraculous substance which God multiplies as He divides it.

VICTOR HUGO

A MOTHER PRAYS * 24

TEACH ME, LORD

*Teach me, my God and King,
In all things Thee to see,
And what I do in anything,
To do it as for Thee.*

GEORGE HERBERT

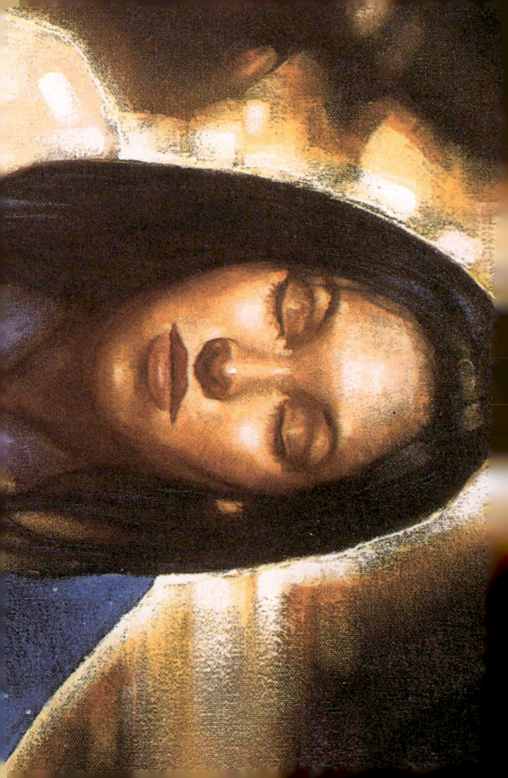

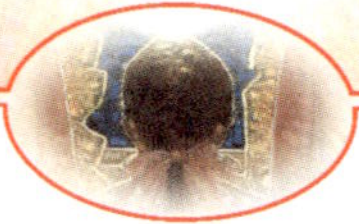

Keep yourself clean and bright—you are the window through which the world sees God.

ANONYMOUS

Dear God, if my children are looking at me trying to see You, then we've got work to do. Help me to show You better in the areas of...

A MOTHER PRAYS

A Parent's Love

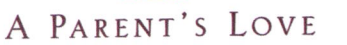

We never know the love of the parent till we become parents ourselves. When we first bend over the cradle of our own child, God throws back the temple door, and reveals to us the sacredness and mystery of a father's and a mother's love to ourselves.

HENRY WARD BEECHER

✵ A MOTHER PRAYS—75 ✵

A MOTHER PRAYS ✳ 26

No man is really old until his mother stops worrying about him.

WILLIAM RYAN

Can a mother forget the baby at her breast and have no compassion on the child she has borne?

ISAIAH 49:15

A MOTHER PRAYS ★ 74

It is one thing to know how God thinks; it is quite another to want what He wants.

JOHN WHITE

Father, not as I will, but as you will.

MATTHEW 26:39

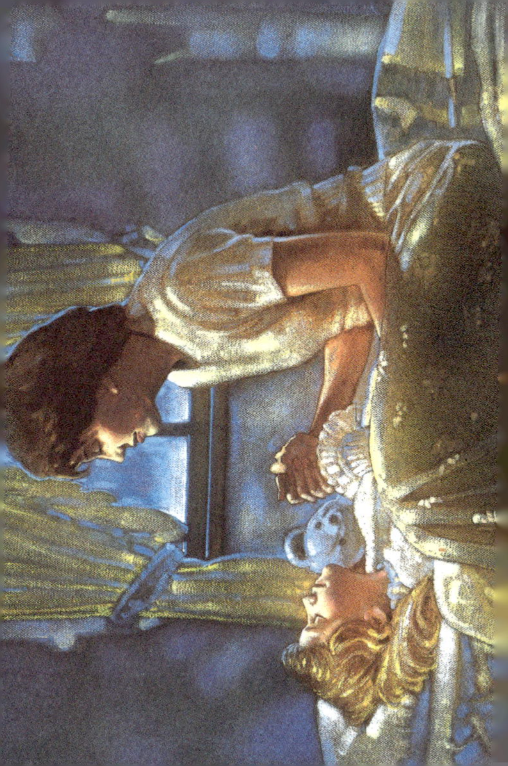

TRANSFORMED BY PRAYER

We are transformed by prayer until our hearts and our lives are suffused by the passion to do the will of God.

E. F. HALLOCK

A Prayer for Today

*H*elp us, God, and give us light so that we don't stand in our own way; let us do from morning till night what should be done, and give us clear ideas of the consequences of our actions.

GOETHE

A MOTHER PRAYS—27

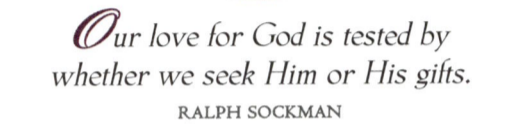

Our love for God is tested by whether we seek Him or His gifts.

RALPH SOCKMAN

But seek first his kingdom and his righteousness, and all these things will be given to you as well.

MATTHEW 6:33

★ A MOTHER PRAYS—72 ★

*W*e have become so engrossed in the work of the Lord that we have forgotten the Lord of the work.

A. W. TOZER

*B*ut as for me and my household, we will serve the Lord.

JOSHUA 24:15

★ A MOTHER PRAYS—28 ★

A MOTHER PRAYS * 71

You cannot teach a child to take care of himself unless you will let him try to take care of himself. He will make mistakes; and out of these mistakes will come his wisdom.

FRANCIS BACON

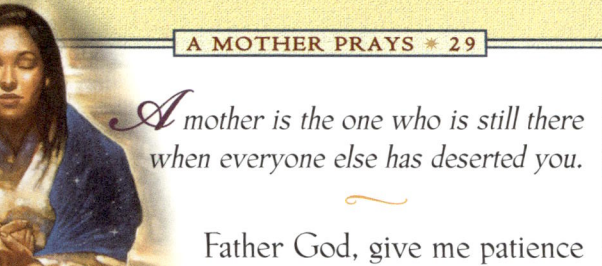

A MOTHER PRAYS * 29

A mother is the one who is still there when everyone else has deserted you.

Father God, give me patience and steadfastness to support my child as he/she...

The Ability to Manage

The energy which makes a child hard to manage is the energy which afterward makes him a manager of life.

HENRY WARD BEECHER

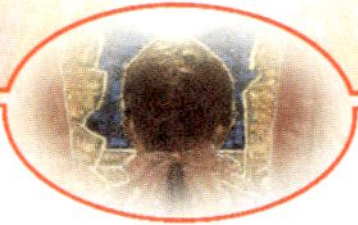

They're Watching

Children are natural mimics who act like their parents in spite of every attempt to teach them good manners.

ANONYMOUS

A MOTHER PRAYS—30

A mother's love perceives no impossibilities.

PADDOCK

Father, some days nearly everything seems impossible. Help me to remember Your power to change me and my child as we...

A MOTHER PRAYS ✻ 31

MOTHER LOVE

The mother love is like God's love; He loves us not because we are lovable, but because it is His nature to love, and because we are His children.

EARL RINEY

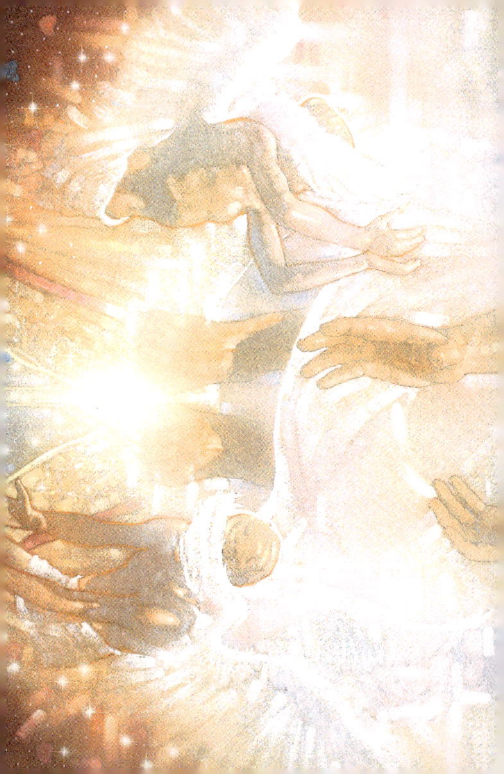

Love is very patient and kind.
1 CORINTHIANS 13:3

Lord, thank You for Your boundless love. Help me to reflect Your love to my child today in…

A MOTHER PRAYS—32

A MOTHER PRAYS—68

God, the blessed and only Ruler, the King of kings and Lord of lords, who alone is immortal and who lives in unapproachable light, whom no one has seen or can see. To him be honor and might forever. Amen.

1 TIMOTHY 6:15, 16

I Tried

Make a rule, and pray God to help you to keep it, never if possible, to lie down at night without being able to say, "I have made one human being, at least, a little wiser, a little happier, or a little better this day."

CHARLES KINGSLEY

A MOTHER PRAYS—33

God does not comfort us to make us comfortable, but to make us comforters.

JOHN HENRY JOWETT

Father, help me to comfort my child today in...

★ A MOTHER PRAYS—67 ★

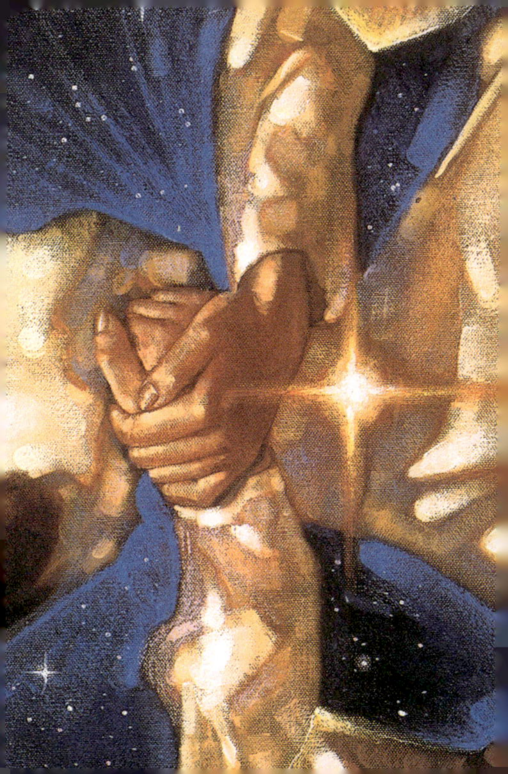

A MOTHER PRAYS · 66

A mother is not a person to lean on but a person to make leaning unnecessary.

— DOROTHY CANFIELD FISHER

Trust in the Lord with all your heart and lean not on your own understanding.

PROVERBS 3:5

A MOTHER PRAYS ★ 34

Keep praying, but be thankful that God's answers are wiser than your prayers!
— WILLIAM CULBERTSON

Dear God, I ask for Your will for my family as we...

Fill the Bucket

Parents need to fill a child's bucket of self-esteem so high that the rest of the world can't poke enough holes to drain it dry.

ALVIN PRICE

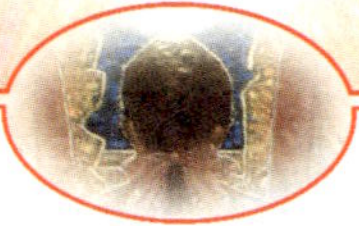

The importance of grandparents in the life of little children is immeasurable. A young child with the good fortune to have grandparents nearby benefits in countless ways. It has a place to share its joys, its sorrows, to find a sympathetic and patient listener, to be loved.

A MOTHER PRAYS • 64

Our lives are a manifestation of what we think about God.

Lord, my children are watching me. They see what I really believe by how I act. I desperately want to show them the real You, but I'm struggling with...

A MOTHER PRAYS ✻ 36

Being a mother enables one to influence the future.

JANE SELLMAN

And the things you heard me say in the presence of many witnesses entrust to reliable men who will also be qualified to teach others.

2 TIMOTHY 2:2

HE DOES ANSWER

In the midst of your doubts, don't forget how many of the important questions God does answer.

VERNE BECKER

I need to stop talking about prayer—and pray.

BERTHA MUNRO

Lord, help me to pray with my children today about...

True prayer is a way of life, not just in case of an emergency.

Father, I know how to pray in crises, but help me and my child to pray more in the good times.

Impress them [My commandments] on your children. Talk about them when you sit at home and when you walk along the road, when you lie down and when you get up.

DEUTERONOMY 6:7

★ A MOTHER PRAYS—38 ★

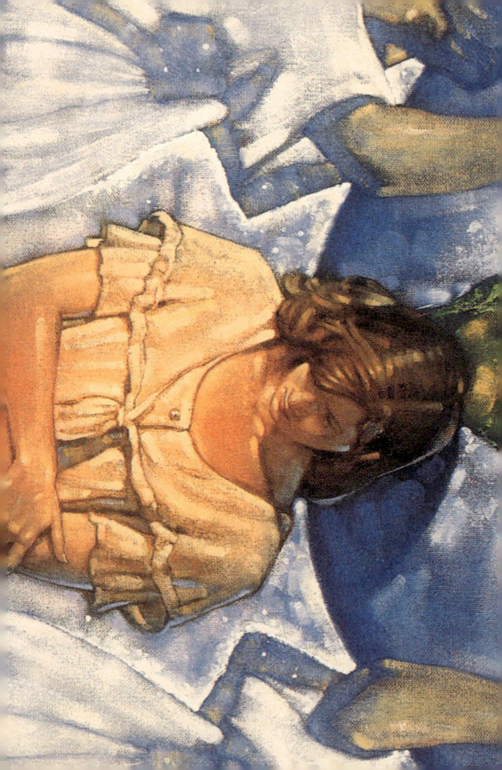

My hands are too tired to hold a torch on high, but they can light a candle in a nursery.

ELLIS MEREDITH

Loving Father, I'm not the wisest or most ambitious mother around, but I love this child. Use me today to teach...

A MOTHER PRAYS—39

A MOTHER PRAYS • 61

HANNAH'S PRAYER

I prayed for this child, and the Lord has granted me what I asked of him. So now I give him to the Lord. For his whole life he will be given over to the Lord.

1 SAMUEL 1:25–28

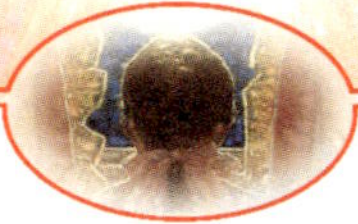

I Asked God

I used to ask God to help me.
Then I asked if I might help Him.
I ended up by asking Him to do
His work through me.

—JAMES HUDSON TAYLOR

A MOTHER PRAYS—40

A Little Bit of Heaven

Blessed be childhood, which brings down something of heaven into the midst of our rough earthliness.

HENRI FRÉDÉRIC AMIEL

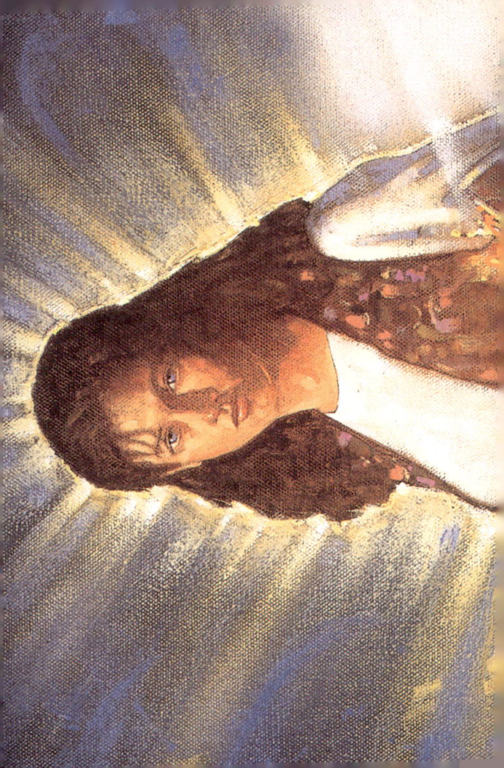

A MOTHER PRAYS ✳ 59

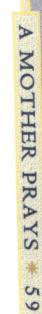

A Christian mother sees more on her knees than a philosopher on his tiptoes.

Heavenly Father, parenting books are good, but I seek Your wisdom on the child development issue of...

I long to put the experience of fifty years at once into your young lives, to give you at once the key of that treasure chamber every gem of which has cost me tears and struggles and prayers, but you must work for these inward treasures yourselves.

HARRIET BEECHER STOWE

The only lasting treasure is spiritual; the only perfect freedom is serving God.

MALCOLM MUGGERIDGE

But store up for yourselves treasures in heaven.

MATTHEW 6:20

✷ A MOTHER PRAYS—58 ✷

The best measure of spiritual life is not ecstasies but obedience.

OSWALD CHAMBERS

God, help me to teach my child to obey You first, and then all others in positions of authority including me and...

★ A MOTHER PRAYS — 42 ★

Never be afraid of giving up your best, and God will give you His better.

HINTON

Dear God, thank You for being so generous to our family. Help me to be a giver and to teach my child to be a giver.

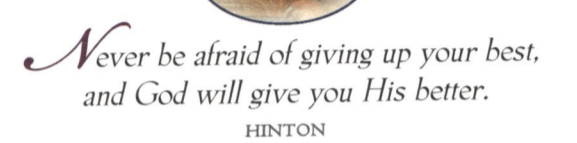

★ A MOTHER PRAYS—57 ★

God has conferred upon us a great honor: that of laboring together with Him. It is ours to bring the word that will create new life, build a new society, and make life more livable, and make Christ live again among men.

— A. P. GOUTHEY

A MOTHER'S FAITH

I have been reminded of your sincere faith, which first lived in your grandmother Lois and in your mother Eunice and, I am persuaded, now lives in you also.

2 TIMOTHY 1:4, 5

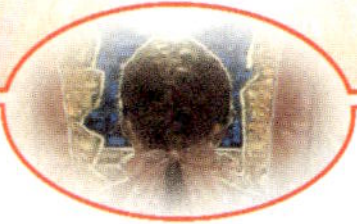

An anxious heart weighs a man down,
but a kind word cheers him up.
PROVERBS 12:25

Father, help me to remember this verse
and to speak kind words to my children today.

✴ A MOTHER PRAYS—44 ✴

A Baby Is...

A baby is a small member of the family that makes love stronger, days shorter, nights longer, the bank roll smaller, the home happier, clothes shabbier, the past forgotten, and the future worth living for.

A MOTHER PRAYS ✳ 45

*W*hen praying, we should not give God instructions. God listens to prayer, not advice.

ANONYMOUS

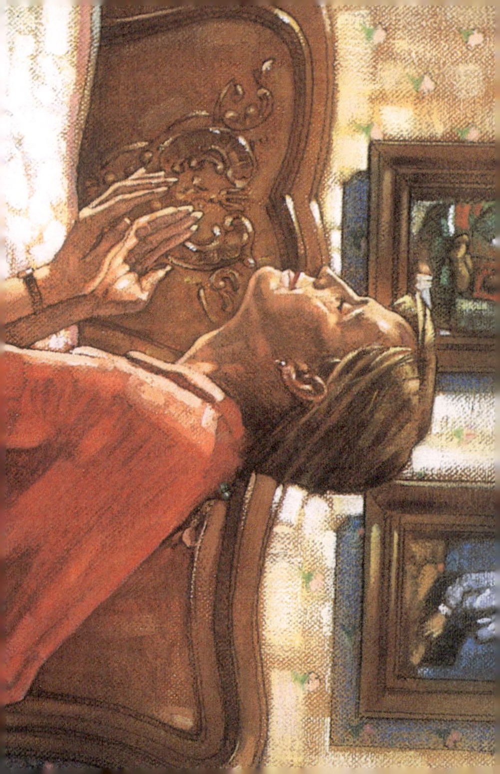

Some are kissing mothers and some are scolding mothers, but it is love just the same, and most mothers kiss and scold together.

PEARL S. BUCK

Love and faithfulness meet together, righteousness and peace kiss each other.

PSALM 85:10

A MOTHER PRAYS—46

Prayer is not getting but becoming.

SIDNEY GREENBERG

Lord, I want to become more than I am now.
I want to become more like You in...

PREPARED TO LIVE

Our greatest obligation to our children and grandchildren is to prepare them to understand and to deal effectively with the world in which they live—not with the world we have known—or the world we would prefer to have.

GRAYSON KIRK

A MOTHER PRAYS—47

He Dares Us

As we cry to God, He hears, and dares us to look at things from His perspective.

KAREN BOSCH

A MOTHER PRAYS—53

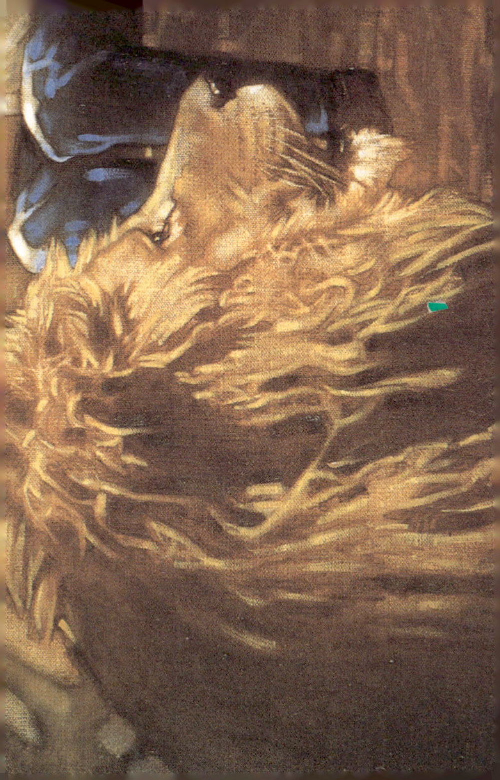

A MOTHER PRAYS * 52

Nothing makes one feel so strong as a call for help.

— GEORGE MACDONALD

Lord, I confess my complete and utter need for You, especially in...

A MOTHER PRAYS * 48

It is impossible for that person to despair who remembers that his Helper is omnipotent.

JEREMY TAYLOR

Great is our Lord and mighty in power.

PSALM 147:5

How to Mother

Learning how to be a mother is not a matter of adopting a certain set of attitudes, but of expressing one's own personality in the task of responding flexibly to the child's needs.

SHEILA KITZINGER

What the mother sings to the cradle goes all the way down to the coffin.

HENRY WARD BEECHER

Dear Father, I want to use this influence You have given me. Help me and my child to praise Your...

A MOTHER PRAYS—49

GOD'S PREACHERS

Children are God's apostles, day by day sent forth to preach of love, and hope, and peace.

JAMES RUSSELL LOWELL

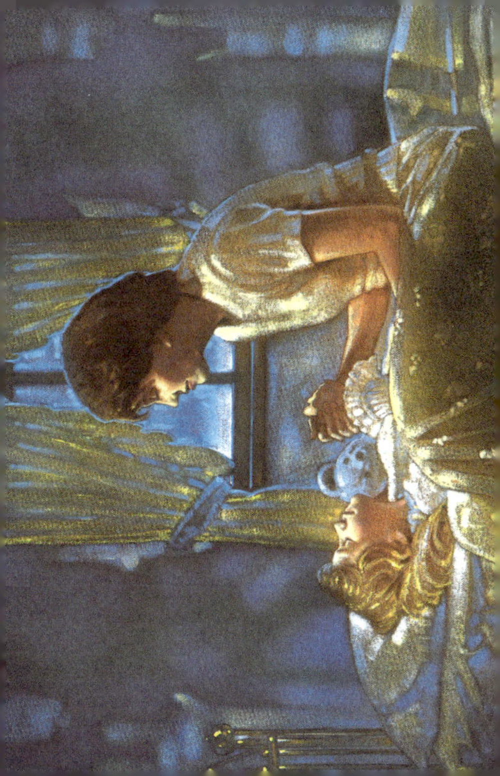

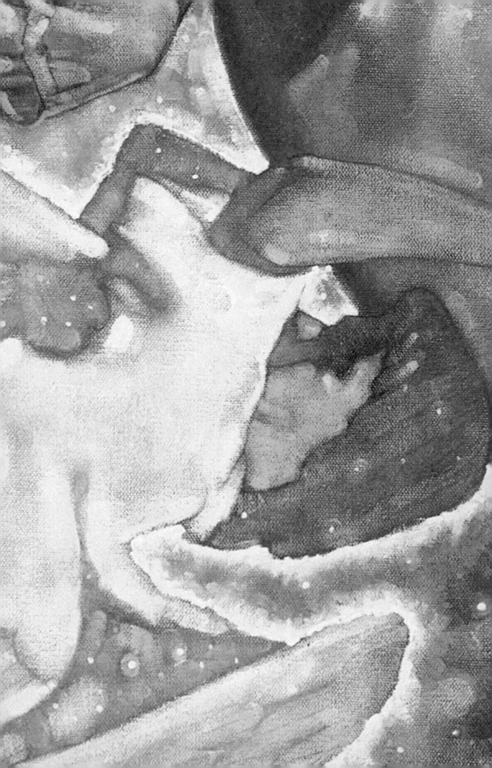

A MOTHER PRAYS

101 Thoughts and Prayers